NOW

Series Preface

The volumes in this 7" x 4" series published by New City Press offer a meditation a day for four weeks, a bite of food for thought, a reflection that lets a reader ponder the spiritual significance of each and every day. Small enough to slip into a purse or coat pocket, these books fit easily into everyday routines.

Máire O'Byrne

NOW

This Moment Matters
at home, work, church, school...

NEW CITY PRESS
of the Focolare
Hyde Park, NY

Published in the United States by New City Press
202 Comforter Blvd., Hyde Park, NY 12538
www.newcitypress.com
©2014 Máire O'Byrne

Cover design by Durva Correia

Library of Congress Cataloging-in-Publication
Data on file.

ISBN: 978-1-56548-500-6

Printed in the United States of America

Contents

one
The Present Moment
Lived in the Family

two
The Present Moment
Lived in the Workplace

three

*The Present Moment
Lived in the Parish*

four

*The Present Moment
Lived at School*

Introduction

$\mathcal{A}$re you among the many who are trying to put the gospel message of love into practice but don't know where to start? Do you, instead of attending to your current task, allow yourself become distracted about things that have happened in your past or that might happen in your future? If your answer to these questions is "yes" then this little book may help. It considers, through reflections and experiences, how "the present moment" can be lived in the family, the workplace, the parish and among young people.

What is "the present moment"? Sometimes referred to as "the here and now" or simply as the "now," the present moment is commonly understood as that period of time that falls between the past and the future. When put into practice it can bring about an inner state of peace that, in turn, brings more clarity, calmness and positivity to the task at hand.

To ask how we can live in the present moment is to ask how we can live in God, since only God lives in the eternal "now" (see Ex 3:14). Although it is very difficult for us human beings to understand how we can live in God our belief that it is possible is repeatedly confirmed by the many experiences found within the pages of this book.

What are the benefits of living in the present moment? The extent to which we experience unhappiness and anxiety is usually proportionate to the amount of time we allow ourselves regret something about our past or fear something about our future. While this behavior inevitably results in negative feelings like resentment, hurt, dissatisfaction or judgment, we still continue to spend our mental energy on things that cause us interior turmoil. If we truly want to replace this pattern of behavior with a trust in God's mercy and providence, then now is the time to begin. The more we live each present moment the more we enter into what Augustine called a "now-standing-still," a place where we "meet" God within ourselves, in each neighbor and also between us (see Mt 18:20).

Difficult? Yes. Worthwhile? Certainly. Why not give it a try and, if at first you don't succeed don't be discouraged. Simply try again. As the experiences reported here attest it is not only possible but it can have beneficial effects on those who practice it and, consequently, for all those we meet throughout the course of our daily lives.

The Present
Moment
Lived in the
Family

1 God's Providence

"And can any of you by worrying add a single hour to your span of life?"

Mt 6:27

Reflection

In his Gospel, Matthew tells us that God intervenes in our individual lives in an all-loving, all-wise and all-encompassing way (see 6:25-34; 10:29-31). When we choose to live our lives in accordance with this belief we find that God does indeed intervene, often when we least expect it and in the most surprising ways. Like a faithful, steadfast and ever-present companion, God's intervention not only brings great comfort along the journey of life but also instills a desire to reciprocate, to be an instrument of this providence for others. When our lives reflect joy, especially amid suffering, we witness to a God who is continuously present and who always finds ways to reveal himself in and through those who help us in our everyday lives.

Experience of Life

Husband: While on a recent vacation my wife and I were lugging our two suitcases from the subway entrance to the platform. Problem was, we wound up on the wrong platform. We needed to go back up the stairs, cross over the tracks and then down the other side. Because of a recent surgery I couldn't help my wife with our luggage. I felt bad about that, but I knew there was one thing I could do — to swallow my embarrassment and immediately give the problem over to God.

Wife: As I stood there on the platform I began to worry - could I manage to carry the bags up and down the stairs again and would we miss the train? But I decided to stop these thoughts and, instead, to focus on the here and now and take one step at a time. Just as we turned to make our way back up the stairs, it seemed out of nowhere, two men came along, lifted our cases and carried them to the correct platform.

T. & R. O'S.

Questions

1) When have you lived in the present moment?

2) How can living in the moment save you from unnecessary worry?

2 *Lived Collectively*

"[T]he present of past things is memory, the present of present things is attention, and the present of future things is expectation."

St. Augustine[1]

Reflection

What counts for us Christians is not what we do or don't do but how we live each present moment. If, in place of organizing activities, of trying to achieve this or that result, we agree together to root ourselves in the present moment then we will inevitably find ourselves enabled by the Holy Spirit to take care of each detail as it presents itself. How we smile, listen, prepare a meal, drive the car, write a letter or share a joy will take on a new and fuller dimension. As well as being witnesses to the power of love lived collectively, living like this can serve to fortify our own belief in God's forgiving compassionate love, a love that swallows up every disharmony in his ever-greater mercy.

Experience of Life

We have been married for nine years. My wife is German and I am American, and all our family live overseas. My wife's brother lives in Germany and recently we visited him because we wanted to spend time with him. Being with him is never easy, as he and my wife have a difficult family history. He can be generous, relaxed and friendly and then can be moody, silent and hostile. Sometimes trying to be loving and caring annoys him and it's difficult to know how to be with him. On the last visit, we decided together that we would live each situation as it came, trying to live each moment well and to show him our love. The visit together was transformed, as we were more relaxed and not constantly "walking on eggshells." Rather, as an expression of our unity and listening to the Holy Spirit in each moment, we were able to love him and live the time together, simply and freely. Sometimes he went off on his own and we met up later, always relaxed and open to the next moment. At the end, he was very happy and sent us a postcard, thanking us again for the great weekend we shared together.

D. & A. F.

Questions

1) How does the Holy Spirit help you live in the present?

2) When have you realized God's mercy because you were trying to live in the present?

3 Reaching Out

"Now only one thing matters: not to miss the present moment, the only thing we really have in our hands."

Chiara Lubich[2]

Reflection

Among the many challenges facing families today are the difficulties presented by being scattered around the world in different countries. Unable to be physically present to each other, and so not in a position to help out in "the present moments" of everyday life, those who find themselves in this position can show their love for one another by entrusting each other, in all those present moments, to God's loving mercy. The fact that we cannot live in each other's time and place can help us become more aware that we are all children of God, of the one Father who desires that we reach out in love not only to our biological family but also to each neighbor who in any given moment may need our love.

Experience of Life

Because our son was being bullied in school we decided to relocate to another part of the city. Within a few months we noticed that our son had grown more confident and happy. Then, just as life was resuming some normality, the world economic crisis began to seriously affect my husband's work. Shortly after we had settled into our new home he was asked to spend every week, from Monday to Friday, on the road. Humanly speaking this couldn't have come at a worse time as our son, who was now a teenager, needed his dad more than ever. Yet my husband needed to earn a living. The only way we were able to take this step was by focusing on each moment as it passed before us, trusting that God would look out for us. This all happened two years ago and while it's been difficult it has enriched each of us in different ways, making us stronger and more united as a family.

B.H.

Questions

1) What can you do to help yourself live in the present moment?

2) What does "the present moment is the only thing we have in our hands" mean to you?

4 *Enlarge Our Hearts*

"He who lives in the present lives eternally."

Ludwig Wittgenstein[3]

Reflection

When we get the opportunity to accompany loved ones as they prepare for eternal life we can find ourselves placing great value on every moment we spend with them. Aware that our time together is limited we give great importance to their every word and gesture. Every moment takes on a heightened significance and becomes locked into our memories. Although often unable to do anything to alleviate the person's physical suffering, we can help create an atmosphere of love so that this final stage of their life is eased. One of the ways we can do this is to enlarge our hearts so that our love is not only directed at the person who is dying but also at the others who, in that moment, may be next to us.

Experience of Life

Some time ago, when I had moved to a country far from where I had grown up, I got a phone call from my mother telling me my dad was in intensive care. Not fully comprehending what I had been told, I immediately phoned some friends who came right away. As soon as they arrived it was as if they were my sisters and my father was their father too. They helped me pack a suitcase, drove me to the airport and gave me the foreign currency I would need. With each act of love they helped calm me down to the point where I could entrust everything to the love of God. Agreeing with them to take one step at a time, I arrived safely and immediately found a taxi driver who knew exactly where I needed to go, even to the brain injury unit at the hospital – he had been there many times with his son! Through every stage of my dad's dying I felt the love and prayers of my friends helping me stay in each present moment, to be there for my mother, and to believe in the love of God for my dad.

M.A.

Questions

1) When has living one moment at a time helped you cope with a particular difficulty in your life?

2) What impact does living one moment at a time have on life eternal?

5 Beyond Time

> "Truly I tell you, unless you change and become like children, you will never enter the kingdom of heaven."
>
> *Mt 18:3*

Reflection

Contemplating life with childlike simplicity and clarity is a wondrous thing. It situates us in the "now," where no one has any more or less time than anyone else. Whether we are old or young we all share in the same time element, that of the present moment. Convinced that we don't have time for this, that, or the other thing, adults usually don't allow themselves the time to contemplate how they can best live in the here and now and so often miss out on the unique and precious gift waiting to be unwrapped in each present moment. Sometimes, simply by watching like a child, we can "touch" what is beyond time: eternity. We can get a sense of time as standing still, a time that has no past or future and in which every moment is new and inviting, just waiting to be discovered.

Experience of Life

In my retirement I'm tempted to live in the past. One afternoon my wife asked me to take a walk with her, but I felt tired and my arthritis was acting up. But my wife, who is a nurse, reminded me how important it was for me to walk. In that present moment I took her advice. We drove down to Brooklyn Bridge Park, and I walked a bit then had to rest. I sat watching the tugboats and barges, the water taxis and sailboats pass by, reminiscing about my childhood; but then I said to myself: "How can I live the gospel right now?" It occurred to me that I might pray for each person who was passing by. I started saying the rosary, praying for all the people on the river. Then I looked up at the Freedom Tower. At first I began thinking of my days as an apprentice plumber working in the skeletons of unfinished skyscrapers, but then noticed the men working on that huge building. I prayed for them too, especially those guys riding on the outside elevator that looked like a little birdcage as it rose to the top. After a while, I felt I was no longer a mere spectator but a fellow-worker on that enormous skyscraper. Living the present moment — no matter where I am — helps me lift myself up from the banal and private to a real adventure. I feel I am doing what God wants me to do.

T.H.

Questions

1) When has a child's perspective helped you live in the present moment?

2) How can living the present moment help you prepare to enter the kingdom of heaven?

6 A Place to Meet God

"Don't wait for time, for time isn't waiting for you."

St. Catherine of Siena[4]

Reflection

It is only in the immediacy of each "now" that we can truly experience and come to know the reality of God. When we choose to ground our response to his divine initiative in faith, then our experience of that particular moment changes. Instead of being just another moment in time, each "now" becomes a place where we "meet" God. These "meetings" can be moments when God challenges us to reshape our lives. Perhaps he wants us to replace the futility of worrying about all those things we can't change (see Lk 12:7), whether they relate to the past or the future, with a stronger awareness of his sustaining presence. To do this we need to persevere and, in place of discouragement, continuously renew our resolve to keep our focus on him. The more we learn to do this the more our present moments will be permeated with his divine presence.

Experience of Life

Over the thirty-four years of our married life we've seen our five children grow into independent individuals. Their different life choices have led them all to live in different countries. While it has been a great joy to see each of them pursue their dreams, it has also yanked on my emotions. Just before our three daughters went their separate ways I went shopping with them. We had lunch together and were having a great time when a thought came to me suddenly: "My God, when will this happen again? Why can't I enjoy moments like this every month, like others I know?" Then I realized that, by jumping out of this lovely moment and feeling sorry for myself, I was missing out on something really special. I quickly detached myself from the "what ifs" of the future and brought myself back into making the most of loving in that precious little moment.

S.O'B.

Questions

1) Since everything worthwhile takes effort, what should you change in order to persevere in living the present moment?

2) How does living in the present moment give witness to your Christian faith?

7 Love that Bears Fruit

"In this moment God and man meet in the Incarnate Word."

George A. Maloney[5]

Reflection

In his first letter John tells us that "God is love" (4:8) and in his gospel he reminds us that Jesus commands us to live in him: "Abide in me as I abide in you" (15:5). Since both of these scriptural verses are rooted in the present tense we can only incarnate them in the present, that is, we can only abide in God, in Jesus, who is love, in the present. Only when we live in the present can we recognize and love Jesus in each one we meet. Only when we live in the here and now can we live the joys and sufferings of the other as if they were our own. Only in every "now" can we, without waiting for the other to love us, be the first to love. In other words, only by loving our neighbor like this in every present moment will they feel themselves wanting to respond in kind. Then, when this happens, we will have Jesus' risen presence in our midst (see Mt 18:20) and, in him, "bear much fruit" (Jn 15:5).

Experience of Life

One Saturday my husband and I had agreed to join some friends from noon until 2 in the afternoon. We were both looking forward to it, but they lived an hour away, so we needed to leave by 11. I started some housework early and was hoping to go to Mass at 10 so I could run some errands after we got back. I could see that my husband was also worried about dropping off recycling while the center was open and completing other things before we left. His concerns were making him anxious and harried. I realized that I could get to Mass later in the afternoon, even though it would take time away from all the other things I wanted to complete. If I took the step to stay in the present, I was sure I'd be able to do what mattered — to love him and do the will of God. It took me a while to take that step but finally I said to him, "Listen, don't worry about rushing around. Nothing is worth getting this anxious over. Let's just work together to make sure we leave peacefully at 11. We're exhausting ourselves before we even get to our friends." I could tell he was relieved and I felt a deep freedom from having taken a step to live not my own "agenda" but to love my neighbor, which is what God was asking of me. I didn't get home from Mass and the other errands until 8 that evening, but instead of weariness I felt the peace that comes from doing whatever was in front of me without rushing, without worry, completely focused on what God wanted from me in the here and now.

J.P.

Questions

1) When has living in the present moment helped build your relationship with God and with your neighbor?

2) How can you figure out what God wants from you in any given moment?

The Present Moment Lived in the Workplace

two

1 _A Delicate Reality_

> "There's only one way of making a success out of your life. It's to give the best that is in you in the framework of the present moment by personally responding to the love of the God present in this situation."
>
> _Michel Quoist[6]_

Reflection

The present moment is a delicate reality. It needs to be handled with care because it is only in the "now" of our human history that we find our point of contact with God. These moments are like annunciations in our lives which, while summoning us to detach from everything that belongs to the past or the future, call us to place ourselves totally at God's disposal. Although of such short duration, these moments are all that count because without them we cannot attend to the work at hand. The more we remain faithful to our commitment to live our lives in accordance with what God asks of us in every given moment, the more the Son is made flesh in us and, through us, continues his Father's creative and redemptive plan.

Experience of Life

Recently I found out that personal circumstances would require me to leave my job. My boss wasn't available that week, so I had an extra few days to worry both about whether I would manage to get my various tasks done before leaving and about my boss's reaction to my unexpected departure. Instead of worrying though, I tried to focus on my work, moment by moment, trusting that if I did this God would ensure that all would turn out for the best. When the boss finally did come back it turned out – to my amazement – that both he and the rest of the staff were very supportive of my move. They went out of their way to express great appreciation for my contributions over the few years I had worked for them. I learned not to worry about what 'might' happen, and the value of focusing on what is in front of me, moment by moment.

D.O'B.

Questions

1) If our lives are made up of a succession of moments, what can you do to live in the here and now?

2) Why does God want you to live in the present moment?

2 Freedom

> "[W]hen you will no longer see yourself in any moment, then you will be free."
>
> *Igino Giordani*[7]

Reflection

Freedom, understood in a secular sense, can mean the power of self-determination, the ability to choose and follow any particular course of action that suits our individual requirements. For St. Paul, however, freedom signifies the capacity to be in relationship with God and one another (see Gal 5:13). Understood in this light, freedom is the God-given ability to shift the focus off our own individual concerns by putting it, instead, onto the needs of our fellow human beings. Realistically, we can only exercise this ability, especially in situations when our neighbor is annoying us, moment by moment. Fidelity to this process demands both a generous heart and a strong commitment. A generous heart because it is not easy to be more concerned about the other than about ourselves, and a strong commitment to start again every time we slip back into the arena of our own concerns. It is in moments when we live like this that we put our God-given gift of freedom into practice.

Experience of Life

I am the Director of a language school that offers English classes and related activities for teenagers from all over the world. One morning one of our teachers decided to move her class to another room without letting me know. As a result some students who arrived late were confused when they went to their usual location and did not find their class. I eventually found the class and brought the students there. I felt annoyed with the teacher because she did not consult me about the change. It meant that I was now late for a meeting with a group leader who wanted to discuss some important issues. When I sat down with the group leader I found it really difficult to concentrate on what he was saying as I was still upset with the teacher. But, I realized that I needed to set the incident aside and focus instead on the present moment. When I did this I was able to make myself present to the group leader and listen closely to everything he had to say.

A.B.

Questions

1) When have you, by living in the here and now, grown in your relationship with God?

2) What does the present moment have to do with freedom?

3 Peace

"One thing alone is beautiful, lovable, attractive, useful, radiant: what God wants of you in the present moment."

Chiara Lubich[8]

Reflection

The more we root ourselves in the present, not allowing our minds drift into the past or the future, the more we are able to perceive God's presence in all the little moments of each day. Those who choose to live in the here and now learn to endure with forbearance the delays and troubles that confront them as they go about their daily tasks. Not allowing our limitations to distract us from the task at hand, instead choosing to entrust them to God, inevitably strengthens our belief in a God who loves us despite our shortcomings. Rather than moments of disquiet, such times in our lives can become moments where we can, by relaxing into God's loving presence, go about our daily tasks in peace.

Experience of Life

In my work as a dispensing optician, whenever I'm with a client, the most important thing for me is to look after that person's needs. So as to let patients know I care, I try to give them my undivided attention one moment at a time. On one occasion I was interrupted by a colleague who wanted me to do something for him after my consultation. Multi-tasking is not my forte, and the interruption made me feel agitated. I just wanted to ignore his request and ask him to come back later. Instead, I decided to trust that God would give me the strength I needed to stay focused on the present moment. As soon as I took this step, my agitation was replaced with a sense of peace and I found myself able to be pleasant to my colleague while also being able to attend to my patient.

H.B.

Questions

1) When has living in the present moment strengthened your belief in God's love for you?

2) What does God want of you in this present moment?

4 *Possibilities*

"Let us live the present moment and in the present do the work of mercy which God asks from us."

Chiara Lubich[9]

Reflection

It is through the door of the present moment that God enters into our lives and, when we open it and receive him, he enters through us into the lives of those around us. Lasting as it does only as long as the wink of an eye each moment is, nonetheless, pregnant with possibility. Not letting ourselves be burdened by the past or the future allows us concentrate more easily on all the "nows" of each day, on all the present moments that we have been given. Each of these narrow passages of time affords us an opportunity for meaningful action which, while always taking a different form, allows us speak and act as if our words and actions were our last. Such being the case, our words and actions have a greater chance of bringing some joy and peace into the lives of those who cross our daily path.

Experience of Life

When I stepped outside to take a break, I passed a woman sitting in a wheelchair. I tried to make eye contact, but she was wearing earphones and her face looked tired and sad, blank. I moved on, but then I stopped. Isn't she someone from my parish? I wasn't sure, and she seemed shut off in her own world. Still, I decided to turn back. I approached and said loudly enough to get her attention, "Excuse me, do you go to St. Timothy's?" "Yes!" We began talking about the parish, and then she proceeded to tell me about her life, challenges with her family, most of whom had stopped going to church. She shared the serious issues she was facing with her grandchildren and how she was trying to help them, even though other family members mocked her efforts and her faith. A half hour passed very quickly. Just as I began to tell her something I had read about the importance of grandparents, her grandson came to pick her up. He recognized me from the church. Before they left, I told both of them about how grandparents can provide role models of successful, fulfilled lives, such as she and her husband who had stayed together for fifty years. Her grandson agreed. "That's right, Grandma!" She was vibrant and smiling as they left. I was thankful I had not let that dear person pass by me in vain!

M.L.

Questions

1) How does living the present moment help you develop a friendship with God?

2) How would your life change if you treated every moment as if it were your last?

5 Conscience

"[Y]our every moment should be a flash of fire, the fire of duty, obedience, and patience."

Francis Xavier Nguyen Van Thuan[10]

Reflection

How are we to understand Jesus' command to "Give to the emperor the things that are the emperor's, and to God the things that are God's" (Mk 12:17; Mt 22:21)? While this particular command draws together the secular and religious elements of our lives it, like all of Jesus' teachings, is situated in the context of the present moment. This being so, perhaps we can say that Jesus not only wants us to pay our taxes and attend to our religious duties but that he also wants us to treat the secular and the religious elements of our lives cohesively and to do so in every present moment. Applying this understanding to the work situation means that our business decisions are not limited to the profit motive but are informed moment by moment by the dictates of conscience.

Experience of Life

Sam: I was approaching twenty-one years with the same company, making a good salary, and receiving good benefits. I felt secure despite rumors that our department was going to close, but that was exactly what happened. All the staff of our department were assigned to a placement center for sixty days. During the first few days, I had an interview within the company. It went well, but as I walked out the door a little voice from inside kept saying, "What that department is involved in is unacceptable to your beliefs." This reaction caught me completely by surprise, because I had worked in the very same division when I began with the company and thought nothing of it. But I had since made the choice to put God in the first place in my life and I couldn't turn my back on him now. I talked it over with my wife, Rita, and we agreed that I should not take this particular job, which would have given me the same pay, benefits, and security to which we had become accustomed. As twenty years of hard work and dreams — all our security — vanished, our whole family turned to God.

Rita: When Sam and I sat down to discuss the job offer, the security was tempting, but we really felt that God was asking us to say yes by turning our backs on material worries and placing ourselves in his hands, trusting in his providence.

S. & R. J.

Questions

1) How does living in the present enhance the secular and religious elements of your life?

2) How does living in the here and now help inform your conscience?

6 Starting Again

> "From early morning until I go to bed and in all situations of life, I always try to check my motivation and be mindful and present in the moment."

The Dalai Lama[11]

Reflection

Whenever we react blindly to the inevitable obstacles that continue to appear in our lives, we miss out on the only life we have, the one happening right here and now. Allowing our awareness to drift into past grievances or future anxieties can block us from focusing on what God is asking of us right now. As soon as we become aware that we have drifted out of the present moment we can begin again by bringing our center of interest back to what is happening in ourselves and in those around us. Starting again every time we become aware that we have slipped out of the present moment requires a rigorous and committed discipline which, in turn, finds its motivation in those people for whom division with our fellow human beings is intolerable.

Experience of Life

I am the executive director of a non-profit organization. Because of funding cuts, I had to make many difficult decisions that had immediate and tough consequences for my staff and our clients. I began to find myself wide awake at 3.15 every morning. Then I would begin to second-guess my decisions and fret over what was looming ahead. I would tell myself that worrying was not going to change anything, but I kept worrying anyway. This continued for months until I decided to really live in the present moment both night and day. When 3.15 came around and I was awake, I would say to myself, "Yes, this problem needs to be solved, but I can solve it at work. Now, all I can do is accept that this problem exists. Now, I need to sleep." Sometimes I would pray. Sometimes I would simply lie quietly, trying to keep my thoughts simple so I could rest even if I didn't sleep. Sometimes I would read until I was sleepy. I would not, however, focus on the problem. After a couple of weeks of remaining in the present moment even at night, I stopped waking at 3.15. I found that I was making better decisions at work and I was making them more quickly. I wasn't anxious anymore and my sleep continued to improve. My job still requires difficult decisions, but I realized that by staying in the present moment I can do my job well during the day and I can enjoy the time I have for rest in the evening.

L.MacN.

Questions

1) When has living the present moment motivated you to start again?

2) What can you do to help yourself be present in the here and now?

7

The Ripple Effect

"See Jesus in every person you meet in each moment of the day, from morning till night."

Chiara Lubich[12]

Reflection

Living in the present moment and loving one person at a time can transform us into instruments of renewal in society. A person who is loved, especially if unexpectedly and by a stranger, often finds themselves wanting to "spread the love" by loving someone else. This ripple effect, which spreads out in ever-increasing circles, can bring beneficial effects into the lives of countless strangers. Those who choose to shift the focus off their own personal concerns and anxieties and put it onto those who pass them by in any given moment manifest a faith that is rooted in the value of living in the present. By entering into and participating in the lives of their fellow human beings, they can often experience freedom from the stresses and strains that might otherwise determine their actions.

Experience of Life

I was going to a meeting with some city officials and was a little short on time and gas. After I had filled up the tank I found a "gentleman" lying on the ground in front of the store as I entered to pay. His appearance was not the most pleasant and my first thought was to enter from another direction so as to avoid him. Then I thought, "This is the person Jesus put in front of me in this moment and I may never meet him again." When I greeted him he asked for money and I told him I literally had only one penny in my pocket, and would be paying with my credit card. So he asked me to buy him a small Coke. I paid the bill and also bought the drink and gave it to him. I was quite surprised when he did not say "thank you." But then I said to myself, "He owes me nothing; on the contrary his presence here has given me the opportunity to love." That evening when I went to Mass, the gospel was the story of Lazarus and the rich man. I was grateful that I had listened to the inner voice that had invited me to remember to love that "gentleman" in our moment of encounter.

M.C.Y.

Questions

1) How does living in the present moment help you manage your busy schedule?

2) How do you understand the connection between God's name, "I am who I Am" (Ex 3:14) and the present moment?

The Present Moment Lived in the Parish

1

We Are Not Alone

"This is the day that the Lord has made; let us rejoice and be glad in it"

(Ps 118:24).

Reflection

Those of us who put the required effort into living one moment at a time do so because we know, from our experience, it is worth it. When, instead of allowing our minds to wander into the past or the future, we decide to focus our attention on living in the "now," we discover God's loving presence within us. This presence, which is never dormant, recognizes itself in those around us (see Mt 25:40) and wants only to reach out in love. This reaching out, when done moment by moment, can be a peaceful exercise because it brings us in touch with our belief that we are not alone, that God is with us. It is his presence within us that not only makes us capable of being more sensitive to the needs of others but that often draws "the other" to reciprocate in like manner.

Experience of Life

Due to a fairly busy schedule I realized that a house Mass I had organized to be held in a week's time was going ahead, but I had not yet asked my parish priest to put it on his calendar. My concerns about being presumptuous and leaving things to the last minute were distracting, even when I tried to pray at Mass. Would my neglect in some way mar my relationship with the parish priest? Instead of worrying about what might be, I decided to live the present moment and shovel my worries, as if they were red hot coals, into the furnace of God's immense love. An immediate result of doing this was that the words of the Mass became more meaningful than usual. Afterwards I was able to speak with the priest. His understanding helped renew my faith in a God who really does "work," especially when we give him our confidence and remain in his peace without trying to do too many things at once.

I.J.

Questions

1) Which of the ordinary events in your life have you come to appreciate by living in the "now"?

2) Why is giving our worries to God in the present moment psychologically and spiritually healthy?

Loyalty

> "If you picture Time as a straight line along which we have to travel, then you must picture God as the whole page on which the line is drawn."

C.S. Lewis[13]

Reflection

We know full well that we cannot live in the past or the future, only in the present. Knowing that the past and future lie beyond our grasp doesn't always allow us realize that only by living in the "now" can each and every present moment be sanctified, made holy. When we actually do what God wants us to do, especially when this involves letting go of our own well-meaning agendas, in those moments we demonstrate our undivided loyalty to God. By commanding us to "love one another as I have loved you" (Jn 15:12), Jesus demonstrates how we can put flesh on this loyalty, how we can allow each and every "now" to be sanctified.

Experience of Life

Some months ago, I presented to our director of religious education what I thought was a very attractive project for our First Communion students. Her response was enthusiastic but she wasn't free to give it her attention as she needed to take some time off work. When she returned she wanted to tell me all her news. The more we chatted, the more I wanted to remind her about the project, but I knew that what was important was to live in the present, acknowledge her return to our community, and be happy at the possibility of working together again. After our chat, as she walked out the door, she turned to me and said she had noticed my project material in her office that day. We immediately agreed to get together the following week to plan how to put the project into action. For me it was a confirmation of the value of living the present moment well.

M.D.

Questions

1) What is sacred in the "nows" of your life?
2) How does living the present moment demonstrate loyalty to God?

3 Listening

> "Love him! Listen to what he wants from
> you in every moment of your life. Do this
> with all your heart."
>
> *Chiara Lubich*[14]

Reflection

Because we are sensory creatures, we find
it easy to hear the voices of those around us.
Although we are also spiritual creatures we don't
always find it easy to hear the voice of the Holy
Spirit speaking through our conscience. Perhaps
this is so because we don't need to do anything
for the sounds that surround us to register, but
we do need to live in the present moment in order to "listen" to the words, to what lies beneath
what we can hear with our ears. When we do
this we bring our whole selves into play, physical and spiritual, and so do not rely so much on
our immediate reaction. If we live in the present
we can be more patient, tolerant, and merciful,
even finding the strength to deny ourselves (see
Lk 6:29; Mt 5:39) in order to be present to those
who cross our daily path.

Experience of Life

As a Catholic priest I focus on the present moment most pointedly while hearing confessions. At our large downtown church I hear confessions anywhere from one and a half to three hours each weekday. I live the present moment by giving my wholehearted and complete attention to each penitent. I try to treat each of them as I would like to be treated, and to love each of them as I would love Jesus himself. Through my love and attention I want to communicate somehow God's personal love and mercy, one by one. I try to enter into each person's reality by trying to be completely empty of myself, not prejudging but listening closely to their words and tone of voice to the very end. Sometimes during a longer pause between penitents I might read a book or meditate on something, but when someone does enter the confessional I instantly set it aside. Sometimes this demands an almost radical interior "violence" toward myself. It is my way of letting go completely of the past present moment and giving my wholehearted love and attention to each person God has placed before me.

T.E.

Questions

1) When has living the present moment enabled you to "listen" rather than just "hear"?

2) In order to truly listen to the person before you, why must you live in the here and now?

4 *Expectations*

"This very moment I may, if I desire, become the friend of God."

Augustine of Hippo[15]

Reflection

For many of us the world can present itself as so secular that it seems hostile to the gospel's law of love. When, therefore, we meet with our fellow Christians we often have underlying expectations that they "know" how to love. But perhaps we should begin by asking ourselves if we "know" how to love. Is our love simply theoretical or does it incarnate Jesus' command to love in all the present moments of our daily lives? Such an incarnated love does not seek any form of gratitude or recognition for our actions. If it is like that of Jesus, it will be self-giving. True love is focused on the good of the other. And we can't love in the past or the future — only in every "now."

Experience of Life

I usually have a lot on my mind concerning my family, but recently, before going into a meeting with our local parish's finance committee, I resolved to leave my personal issues outside the door and to focus on the business at hand. Listening to the many strongly held ideas that emerged I could see that there was no overall plan. I decided to share my idea of making a budget, but this was not received very well. At that stage the atmosphere was getting a bit tense and I wanted to leave, but then I remembered my earlier resolve and so I brought myself back into the present and tried to focus on what each person was saying. At the end of the meeting I suggested we ask the Holy Spirit for inspiration and immediately the whole atmosphere changed. I was very happy to have remained faithful to my resolve to live in the present.

E.McM.

Questions

1) Why would living in the "now" help you become a friend of God?

2) How does having expectations prevent living the present moment?

5 Rooted in God

> "[A]t the heart of the little way is the capacity to know in any given situation the precise demand of love, how best in the here and now of the present moment to will the good of the other."

Robert Barron
(referring to Thérèse of Lisieux's spirituality)[16]

Reflection

Trying to live in the present moment, in the face of everything that calls us out of it, is a high form of spiritual discipline which, it can be said, forms our gateway into the very life of God (see Jn 17:21). Going beyond what others may think of us and choosing, in the here and now, to put Jesus' commandment of love into practice helps us experience God's peace and joy within ourselves. This marvelous feature of Christian life not only confirms our own faith but also lets us witness to those around us. Those fortunate enough to meet someone whose life is harmonious, with no separation between their faith and their life, regularly feel touched by God's personal love for them. This in turn often motivates them to commit themselves, moment by moment, to a life rooted in God.

Experience of Life

A parishioner told me of a neighbor who was dying of cancer. The man, though Catholic, insisted that he did not want to see a priest. He had been very harsh to his children, and his sons were estranged from him. I decided to stop by his house for a visit. Opening the door, the man's wife immediately confirmed that her husband did not want to see a priest. In that moment, I knew it was important to let go any "ulterior" pastoral motives, even my good intentions regarding his salvation. She invited me in for a cup of coffee with her and her daughter. That was what I now had to live, talking about everything and anything, also about the family's situation. In the course of the conversation the wife suddenly announced: "Well, maybe I'll try and see if he might see you." She returned from his room, telling us that to her amazement he had agreed. In time the man received the sacraments and was reconciled with his sons.

B.L.

Questions

1) Can you offer an example of how the present moment has served as your gateway to union with God?

2) How can living in the here and now help those around us?

A Divine Adventure

> "The 'way' does not belong to you nor is the present under your control. But as step succeeds step, enjoy each moment as it comes and then continue on your 'way.'"
>
> *Basil the Great*[17]

Reflection

Our lives consist in moment by moment divine adventures. In other words, every moment we live on this earth is a moment when God is calling us into an ever-greater union with one another in him (see Jn 17:21). When we allow our Christian faith to penetrate and link all our actions, we can achieve union with each other in him, an appetizing taste of heaven already here on earth. We can reach beyond what might seem like an unending and impenetrable horizon of difficulties and tap into God's strength working within us. Like a wellspring of inner light this strength can, if we allow it, renew and transform all our present moments and help many others do likewise.

Experience of Life

One month, when I had been focusing on a passage from the First Letter of John, "Not in word, but in deed and in truth" (1 Jn 3:18), a friend called to ask a favor. She knew that I take communion every Wednesday to a woman we both know. She had prepared a meal for her but could not deliver it herself, so she asked me to pick it up from her house and deliver it. At first I said no. Then I remembered that Jesus in this person was asking me to love her by saying yes. So I told my friend that I would pick it up in the morning on my way to church. The next morning traffic was heavy, and because of the added errand I arrived just as the priest was beginning the gospel. At first I felt bad but then was reassured because in a way I started Mass before I arrived by loving my neighbor. After Mass I took communion to the lady and gave her the soup that my friend had prepared. She was happy and impressed that I had gone to all that trouble. I really felt that I fulfilled the gospel in that present moment.

A. F.

Questions

1) When have you felt God's strength working within you as you lived the present moment?

2) By living in the here and now, how can we overcome our reluctance to love?

Our Daily Cross

> "In the state of self-abandonment the one rule is the present moment."

Pierre De Caussade[18]

Reflection

Jesus told his disciples "If any want to become my followers, let them deny themselves and take up their cross and follow me" (Mt 16:24). Anybody who tries to live the present moment knows from experience that every "now" contains an opportunity to deny ourselves and to take up our cross. Some seek to avoid these crosses by adopting a casual or an uncommitted lifestyle. But reality has a way of forcing its attention upon us. We need a strong resolve to generate alternative currents within such lifestyles by which in each present moment we can choose to deny ourselves and take up our cross. The more we live in the here and now, the more we will feel God's support until, at a certain point, we will find nothing left to do but allow ourselves be carried.

Experience of Life

I volunteer in the parish office three days a week on my way home from work. For two hours I do filing, prepare Mass cards, and answer the phone. Usually I am alone, leaving the priests free to do other work. One day, a caller asked for the pastor but he was downstairs with a prayer group, so I took the caller's name and number. A few minutes later, however, the same woman called again. She sounded desperate and was crying. It was time to close the office but I could not just drop this lady. I thought of the present moment. If I trusted in God's grace in the present the future would take care of itself. I made a fast change inside and began to listen again, staying on the phone with her for an hour while she told of the agony that she was going through. She was having a complicated pregnancy and her doctor had advised her to go for an abortion. I listened, then shared my own viewpoint. Even though the law allows abortion at any moment during a pregnancy, it is still morally wrong. I told her about my trust in God in the most difficult situations in my own life and suggested that she trust and believe in His love. At the end of the call she said she was keeping her baby. The following day, when the priest called her, she told him, "A lady in the office helped me in my firm decision to keep the baby."

S. P.

Questions

1) When has living the present moment helped you carry your daily cross?

2) Why might it be necessary to abandon your own way of doing things in order to live the present moment?

The Present
Moment
Lived at School

four

The Circulation of Love

> "Christ is an irresistible force within us, uniting us with God at this very moment."
>
> *Meister Eckhart*[19]

Reflection

To love Jesus in everyone we meet (see Mt 25:40) is a moment-by-moment endeavor. If, in our attempt to do this, we rely on our own strength, then our perspective will probably be dominated by their faults and failings. On the other hand, if we "allow" Jesus in us reach out in love to each one who appears before us in every present moment, then everything changes. When this happens it is no longer only we who look and see; it is Jesus in us who looks and sees himself in the other person. Rather than seeing limits, Jesus sees their limitlessness, their endless possibilities. This level of love often ignites in other persons a desire to respond in kind. In bringing together what might otherwise be fragmented, this circulation of love helps build community.

Experience of Life

Sometimes when we are involved in charity work or social projects we can feel our efforts aren't being recognized or they are not making the impact that we had hoped. For example, a few months ago at school, we had lots of ideas on how to raise money for an education project in Africa. We organized a concert but, with only a few days to go, our group wasn't co-operating and I was worried the event would be a shambles. During one of the practices I looked at my fellow students and realized that in this moment they were the presence of Jesus for me. I began making an extra effort with the people around me, and the more I did this the more they began to do the same. Living the present moment totally for this one practice seemed to ensure the concert would be a success. And what a success it was!

C.B.

Questions

1) How is Christ working within you right now?

2) In what communities are you involved? How can living in the "now" help build solidarity in them?

2 Starting Again

"Life Is Hard by the Yard. By the Inch It's a Cinch."

Unknown Author[20]

Reflection

Wanting to do what God wants us to do binds us to the present moment. Whether the task before us requires a high level of expertise or whether it is something very simple, what matters is how we do it. By remaining in every "now," taking care of one detail at a time, we do everything we can to carry out God's will for us. Letting ourselves drift into the past or the future contradicts our efforts; as soon as we become aware of such a lapse, we need to start again. Starting again is a discipline we need to practice over and over. The more we nurture this discipline the more it can help us stay focused on living in the "now," ready to reach out the hand of friendship to the other person before us.

Experience of Life

For my vacation last year I travelled abroad to visit a friend, who is also thirteen. One day her mother brought home a doll-making set. As the instructions were written in a language I couldn't understand, I was just guessing from the pictures how to make the doll, without putting a lot of thought into it. My friend, however, was following each instruction exactly. It seemed to be important to her that she got everything exactly right. Soon she started correcting my doll. By the third time this happened I was beginning to get angry, but suddenly I stopped and I thought "why should I let this upset me? Why not live this moment as best I can?" After this thought I began trying to follow the directions as well as I could. This helped me be more willing to hand my doll over to my friend whenever she wanted to correct it. By not letting my feelings get in the way I was able to build not just a plaything, but a strong relationship with my friend.

M.O'S.

Questions

1) How can you make the moment-to-moment events in your daily experience into opportunities to love?

2) When have you failed in loving in a particular present moment? How might perseverance have helped you succeed?

3 A Focus on Relationship

"Nothing ever happened in the past; it happened in the Now. Nothing will ever happen in the future; it will happen in the Now."

Eckhart Tolle[21]

Reflection

While childhood can be a carefree time, our adolescent years provide an important bridge between childhood and adulthood. In their efforts to express their own identity as distinct from that of their parents, young people often reject their parents' values. Although these years are frequently marked by conflict and confusion they are also marked by a growing understanding of abstract ideas such as responsibilities, rights, freedom, intimacy, privileges, relationships and morality. These changes, which play out on the physical, emotional, mental, and spiritual levels in the lives of adolescents can, when not lived in the context of the present moment, appear overwhelming. But when lived in the here and now, they lead to a better understanding of how God wants them to live their lives so as to bring his plan for them to fulfillment.

Experience of Life

When I was young life was simple. I felt secure in my family, which was very Catholic in its practices. During those years it seemed that nothing could destroy the sense of harmony in our home. Now I'm sixteen, and I'm questioning everything, including my parents' religious beliefs. I do appreciate a lot of the values they have passed on to me but the fact that they continue to insist I go to Mass every week, when I don't see the point, makes me angry and often leads to huge conflicts. For me this contradicts the value of accepting other persons as they are. So as not to upset my younger brothers and sister I try, literally, one moment at a time, to keep my opinions to myself. Even though I find it very hard to keep going to Mass, it does help maintain peace in the house and so it is worth it.

L.O'B.

Questions

1) When you feel disconnected from those around you, how might living the present moment help restore the relationship?

2) In your current circumstances of life, what experiences have you had in your search for truth?

4 *Authentic Human Beings*

> "You're the yes that's hidden at the heart of every no."

Joe McCarrol[22]

Reflection

To live an authentic human life is to be in relationship with God and our fellow human beings. Many of us have learned, from experience, that this is not as easy as it sounds. It requires a willingness to relinquish our desire for observable and measured lives and, instead, to embrace life moment by moment. While this too may sound feasible in practice it is not easy. Choosing to live in the here and now does open us to uncertainty but those who make this choice can discover that these uncertainties contain infinite possibilities waiting to be explored. The more we allow our yes break through our hesitations, refusals, resistance, and complacency, the more authentic we become, available to serve others and so to grow in our relationship with God.

Experience of Life

I have just started my university studies and have had to move away from home. Originally I was hoping to be accepted at a school close to home so I would not have to pay for room and board and could stay close to my friends. But the way things turned out the best option was to move away. So, I decided I would not get upset by this and, instead, use it as an opportunity to plunge myself completely into my new circumstances. Since I arrived I have taken advantage of every new opportunity. I have made some wonderful new friends and learned a lot. This all happened because I decided to live in the present moment. It has been an extraordinary experience, one that I do not regret.

S.H.

Questions

1) When has your "yes" to God been able to break through your "no" because you were living the present moment?

2) How can living in the present moment demonstrate your faith in God?

Our Final Exam

"Life is a trial and at the end it, too, has to pass an exam."

Chiara Lubich[23]

Reflection

Just as schools use exams to determine how well students have mastered the required material, at the end of our life we will be asked to demonstrate how well we have responded to God's offer to participate in his divine life (see 2 Pt 1:4). Because our final exam will consist in God ratifying our own self-judgment, and because he makes his offer to share in his divine life in the present tense, we can assume that we will have to document how well we have mastered living in the present moment. Although we cannot know how this final episode in our earthly lives will work out, we do believe it will take place in the light of God's love and that we ourselves will be our own internal examiners.

Experience of Life

As a young person it's easy to get wrapped up thinking about the next break from my studies or worried about the next exam. But I have found that living the present moment helps keep everything under control. If I live each day as it comes, I not only enjoy it but find it more productive. As an example, I find that studying well a little bit each day, instead of putting it off until the night before and cramming everything in, can really help when preparing for exams. This way, little by little the knowledge builds up and I usually feel prepared to take the exam. I also feel reassured because I believe that what God wants is for me to do my best in each present moment.

E.B.

Questions

1) How can living the present moment help you face the trials of life?

2) How might looking at your own "final exam" as the last "present moment" of your life help you put your entire life experience into perspective?

# *6 Grace*

> "So do not worry about tomorrow, for tomorrow will bring worries of its own. Today's trouble is enough for today."
>
> *(Mt 6:34)*

Reflection

Since we can't change even the smallest fraction of the past or a nanosecond of the future, perhaps it is most sensible to accept what we cannot change and entrust both our past and our future into the hands of our heavenly father. Embedding ourselves in the present does not mean we don't have to plan for the future, but it allows us do so without worrying. God introduced himself to Moses as: "I am who I am" (Ex 3:14). That tells us that he is not a God who lives in the past or the future; his gift of grace can only be given and received in each present moment. To live in the present, welcoming everything that comes our way, is an ongoing challenge but one we can surely face up to.

Experience of Life

For me, living the present moment has really helped — especially this year. I am in my last year of high school and am preparing to go to college. It is so easy to get overwhelmed by the pressure of the future and to be constantly thinking about next year. When the stress of it all gets to me and I begin to panic, I make a conscious decision to live the present moment well. I concentrate on my studies and live each day as well as I can. Before long the pressure lifts off me and I am able to think more clearly, making everything easier.

C.P.

Questions

1) What can you do to center your life more on the here and now?

2) How would your life change if you lived each present moment in a more conscious way?

7 *God's Love*

> "Life is made of nothing but present moments that have worth for those who want to make something of them. It is the present that counts, the fleeting moment that for me, for you, for us, should be seized on the fly and lived through and through."

Chiara Lubich[24]

Reflection

On a clear night we can see the stars glimmering in the darkness, passively adhering to God's will for them and giving great witness to their Creator. We, on the other hand, have been given the gift of freedom, the ability to choose how to live each present moment. To help us do this in accordance with Jesus' command to love one another (see Jn 13:34; Jn 15:12), God sends the Spirit of his Son into our hearts (see Gal 4:6). God is the one who takes the initiative, but our lives achieve their true potential only if, in every "now," we use our freedom to engage with the inner promptings of his Spirit. Living in the present moment is a conscious, active choice. Each moment lived well can serve as a witness to our God-given gift of freedom and so to our Creator's great love.

Experience of Life

One day, after returning tests to my university students, one girl was clearly irritated and started complaining openly, attacking me personally. At first I felt hostile, then I told myself: "Be careful. Love your neighbor, and love your 'enemy' RIGHT NOW." I told her calmly, "Let's talk later." In my office, she apologized. "I'm sorry. My parents — traditional Indian doctors — are putting pressure on me to get excellent grades and go to medical school. I don't want to, but in Hindu culture parents have a lot to say in our future, studies, and marriage." I tried to imagine walking in her shoes. After a while I said, "I think you have to focus on a bigger decision. What is your whole life going to be about, your life's meaning?" She replied directly: "And what is the meaning for you?" I told her: "Do to others as you would have them do to you. Focus on others, not just yourself." I did not know her belief system, so I said, "This is also the connection to the Divine, in us and between us, in our daily life." She gave me a hug and left. Three months later, after the course had finished, we happened to meet in the corridor. Over lunch she told me, "Our conversation had quite an impact on me. Last summer I volunteered at a hospice for people dying of AIDS. It was a real personal growth lesson. Now I know that the meaning of my life lies in living 'Do unto others...' I found the courage to ask my parents not to send me to medical school...and they accepted! I want to become a social worker. Thanks for that 'decisive moment' after a bad test."

M.N.

Questions

1) What is the connection between our gift of freedom and living the present moment?

2) When has a fleeting moment changed your life?

Notes

1. *The Confessions* (Hyde Park, New York: New City Press, 1997), 300.

2. *Here and Now: Meditations on Living in the Present* (Hyde Park, New York: New City Press, 2005), 13.

3. *World and Life as One: Ethics and Ontology in Wittgenstein's Early Thought*, ed. Martin Stokhof (Stanford, CA: Stanford University Press, 2002), 222.

4. *Women's Political & Social Thought: An Anthology*, eds. Hilda L. Smith and Berenice A. Carroll (Bloomington, IN: Indiana University Press, 2000), 38.

5. *Nesting in the Rock* (Denville, NJ: Dimension Books, 1977), 79.

6. *The Christian Response* (Dublin: Gill and Macmillan Ltd., 1965), 87.

7. *Diary of Fire* (London: New City, 1981), 114.

8. *Essential Writings* (Hyde Park, New York: New City Press, 2007), 76.

9. Chiara Lubich Center Archives, "The Fleeting Moment" (Letter to the young girls of the Third Franciscan Order, around 1949).

10. *The Road of Hope: Gospel from Prison* (Hyde Park, New York: New City Press: 2013), 42.

11. *The World of Tibetan Buddhism* (Somerville, MA: Wisdom Publications, 1995), 4.

12. *A New Way* (Hyde Park, New York: New City Press, 2006), 45.

13. *Mere Christianity* (London: Fount Paperbacks, 1977), 144.

14. *A New Way* (Hyde Park, New York: New City Press, 2006), 41.

15. saints.sqpn.com/saint-augustine-of-hippo.

16. *Catholicism: A Journey to the Heart of the Faith* (New York: Image Books, 2011), 210.

17. *Drinking from the Hidden Fountain*, ed. Thomas Spidlik (London: New City, 1992), 39.

18. *An Anthology of Mysticism*, ed. Paul De Jaegher (London: Burns & Oates, 1977), 179.

19. *The Way of Paradox* (London: Darton, Longman and Todd, 1988), 86.

20. *Words of Light*, ed. E. Helene Sherman (Toronto: Little Brown and Company, 1981), np.

21. *The Power of Now* (Novato, CA: New World Library, 1999), 50.

22. Excerpt from an unpublished song, "Pearl of Light." Used with permission.

23. *Meditations* (London: New City, 2005), 95.

24. Cited during Genfest 2012: http://genfest.org/steps-to/. Editors' translation.

Also available in the

same series:

Praying Advent: Three Minute Reflections on Peace, Faithfulness, Joy, and Light,
Joan Mueller, ISBN: 978-1-56548-358-3

Keepsakes for the Journey: Four Weeks on Faith Deepening,
Susan Muto, ISBN: 978-1-56548-333-0

Pathways to Relationship: Four Weeks on Simplicity, Gentleness, Humility, Friendship,
Robert F. Morneau, ISBN: 978-1-56548-317-0

Pathways to God: Four Weeks on Faith, Hope and Charity,
Robert F. Morneau ISBN: 978-1-56548-286-9

Peace of Heart: Reflections on Choices in Daily Life,
Marc Foley, ISBN: 978-1-56548-293-7

His Mass and Ours: Meditations on Living Eucharistically,
Brendan Leahy, ISBN: 978-1-56548-448-1

Forgiveness: Three Minute Reflections on Redeeming Life's Most Difficult Moments,
Joan Mueller, ISBN: 978-1-56548-426-9

To order visit www.NewCityPress.com
or call 1-800-462-5980
or e-mail orders@newcitypress.com

NEW CITY PRESS
of the Focolare
Hyde Park, New York

About New City Press of the Focolare

New City Press is one of more than 20 publishing houses sponsored by the Focolare, a movement founded by Chiara Lubich to help bring about the realization of Jesus' prayer: "That all may be one" (John 17:21). In view of that goal, New City Press publishes books and resources that enrich the lives of people and help all to strive toward the unity of the entire human family. We are a member of the Association of Catholic Publishers.

Further Reading

The Pearl of the Gospel
978-1-56548-495-5 $6.95

5 Steps to Living Christian Unity
978-1-56548-485-5 $4.95

15 Days of Prayer with Dorothy Day
978-1-56548-491-7 $11.95

Gospel in Action   978-1-56548-486-3 $12.95

A New Way   978-1-56548-236-4 $12.95

5 Steps to Facing Suffering
978-1-56548-502-0 $4.95

Polly's Little Kite   978-1-56548-528-0 $11.95

Periodicals
Living City Magazine,
www.livingcitymagazine.com

Scan to join our mailing list for discounts and promotions or go to www.newcitypress.com and click on "join our email list."